The Essential Guide to the SAT

Hampton Tutors is an academic coaching and tutoring agency, based in Seattle, WA.

Edition 1

Copyright Hampton Tutors, LLC

Email: hello@hamptontutors.com

Website: www.hamptontutors.com

SAT is a registered trademark of the College Board, which is not affiliated with this book.

HH

HAMPTON
TUTORS

CONTENTS

WELCOME

The SAT is not a test of intelligence. It doesn't test creativity, analysis nor even how well you will do at college.

It only tests how good you are at taking the SAT.

Because the SAT is a standardized test, it has standardized questions, and therefore standardized answers. It's highly unlikely the SAT will give you left-field questions or information you've never seen on previous tests.

The purpose of this book is to show you how you can, as efficiently as possible, master the content of the SAT and then use the best technique to approach the test. This book is designed for efficiency.

There's no information in this book that isn't useful for the SAT, and there's no information useful for the SAT that isn't in this book. That's why we call it the *Essential Guide.*

So read this book, practice, and learn the advice to find the best approach for you.

Good luck!

HOW TO PREPARE FOR THE SAT

Begin preparing for the exam as early as you can; a year ahead of time is not too soon.

Plan on regular, long-term practice rather than relying on short-term cramming.

Unless you know you are going to take a digital version of the test, take *timed* practice sections from a *printed* version of the test.

Whenever possible use the official practice materials available from the College Board and Khan Academy.

Always figure out exactly why you have missed any particular problem; keep a record of what you learn.

If you are not making progress, or hit a plateau, consider hiring a tutor. Make sure the tutor is not just a math or English tutor but one experienced at teaching the SAT.

In the weeks leading up to exam, begin taking *full length, timed* practice tests; aim for at least two or three such "dress rehearsals" for the exam.

Spend the evening before the exam doing something relaxing and enjoyable.

1.
The Reading Section

The Reading Test is the first test on the SAT.

The questions relate to 5 different passages: one from prose fiction, two from social studies, and two from the natural sciences.

The test allows you 65 minutes to answer 52 questions, for an average of 13 minutes per passage.

Some of the questions refer to tables or graphics that accompany the reading.

One of the five passages will involve a pair of readings on similar topics.

Your score on the Reading Test will be combined with your score on the Writing and Language Test for a total Reading and Writing score of 200-800.

WHAT METHOD SHOULD I USE?

As you practice for the SAT, try each of the following methods using a timer in order to determine which one works best — or better yet, come up with your own hybrid.

Remember: what works best is just what works for you.

Method #1: The Natural

The most straightforward approach to taking the test is the obvious one: just read the passage and then answer the questions.

Do this if you prefer something simple and uncomplicated. There are no tricks to remember; you just go right to work.

Don't do this if you are a not a fast worker. Each passage should take an average of 13 minutes. You can consider yourself fast if you are *regularly* finishing each passage with a minute or more to spare.

Don't do this if you want to save time. Using this method, you are likely to spend precious minutes reading and trying to understand parts of the passage that you don't need to know.

Method #2: Skim & Answer

How to do it:

(1)   Quickly skim the text.

(2)   Answer the questions.

(3)   Go back and read some sections in more detail to answer the questions.

In 'skimming', you are reading attentively but selectively, skipping over details when possible in order to figure out the general form and meaning of the passage. This should take about 2 or 3 minutes.

Do this if you want to speed up your timing by not wasting any time reading unnecessary material – but are also quite confident in your overall reading and skimming skills.

Don't do this if you think you might misunderstand the passage from skimming and not fully reading it.

Method #3: Backsolving

The backsolving technique involves previewing the questions, marking the passage, and then reading purposefully in order to answer the questions.

Do this if you are not an especially strong performer on the SAT Reading Test. If you are averaging more than 2 missed questions per section, this might be a helpful approach for you.

Do this if you want to save time. With this method, you won't waste time re-reading, since you are answering questions when you first encounter the relevant material.

Do this if you are having trouble understanding the text. This approach can assist comprehension of difficult passages, since the questions can actually help focus your reading.

Don't do this if you find it distracting to stop and start reading the passage again and again.

Don't do this if you prefer to know what the whole passage is about before you answer any questions. It will be harder to gauge the overall tone of the passage, and you'll need to answer the main idea question last.

Here's how it works:

STEP ONE:

Preview the questions, annotating them as you go.

This annotation consists of two parts:

First, use your pencil to mark the passage according to any line references or locations mentioned in the questions. For example, some questions will ask about the implications of 'remarks made in lines 25-27', or about 'the second paragraph.' You can do this with a line in the margin.

Second, mark more general references to the text in the questions, such as names, concepts, or key ideas.

STEP TWO:

Work through the passage:

Read or skim the passage as you normally would, stopping to answer the questions corresponding to the marked portions of the text.

If you come across part of the passage that corresponds to the other references you have marked in the questions, attempt those questions.

Skip main idea questions as well any questions you are unable to answer in less than a minute, circling the question before you move on.

After you've finished working through the passage in this manner, answer the remaining questions, including any you may have skipped.

Five Point Question Attack Plan

Once you've worked out your general approach to reading the passage, you will still need to attack the specific questions.

Here's how:

```
READ CAREFULLY
PREDICT
ELIMINATE
SKIP
GUESS
```

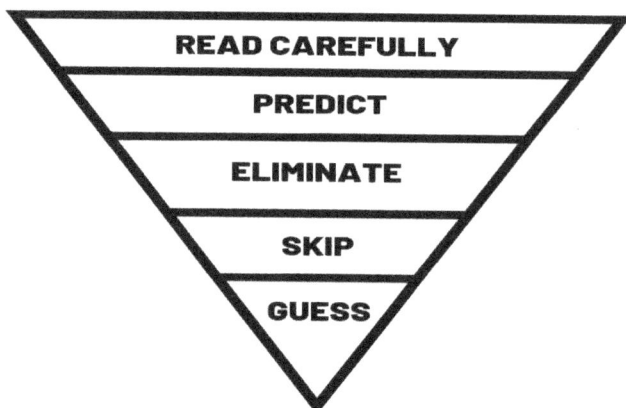

(1) *Read carefully.* Pay attention to every word. Underline important words.

(2) *Predict.* If possible, predict an answer before reading the choices. Sometimes it is helpful to physically cover the options; this forces you to get clear on your understanding of the matter at issue and to avoid a not-quite-right answer.

(3) *Eliminate.* Go through the answer possibilities, using your pencil to

cross out any answers that are definitely wrong.

(4) *Skip.* Consider skipping, circling, and returning later to any questions you cannot confidently answer in less than a minute.

(5) *Guess.* If you don't know the right answer, guess as intelligently as you can.

Expert Test Taking Tips

Now that you've worked out your basic methods, here are some advanced techniques that can help you move up to the next level.

Be a smart guesser.

The answer is not subjective. There is <u>always</u> something that makes an answer right: a key word, phrase, or construction. Find it!

Rely on your reasoning abilities. It is often possible to eliminate one or more options -- or at least show them to be improbable – without reading the passage at all!

Stay close to the main idea. When stuck between two options, choose the one most relevant to the main point of the passage. The SAT Reading Test tends to stay close to the central idea of the passage.

Avoid extremes. When working on questions that concern main ideas, avoid extremes. Hard-to-confirm statements, sweeping generalizations, and other such statements are less likely to be correct.

Take the test in your preferred order.

Read the passages in order of your strength. If you are much better at science oriented passages, for example, you might consider doing the test in reverse order. This helps you to capitalize on your strength and to ensure that you get credit for those answers you are more likely to get right.

Answer the questions within each passage in whatever order works best. Your best order depends on your reading method, but a lot of people like to start with vocabulary and detail questions, saving the more general questions for last.

Manage your time wisely:

Keep an eye on the clock. Always check in after passage 3; you should have at least 25 minutes left.

Don't get stuck. Avoid spending more than a minute on any single question. Guess intelligently and move on to those you can confidently solve. Return to the hard ones if you have time.

Develop a panic strategy. If you are running out of time when you arrive at the final passage, first do the questions you know you can get right (e.g., vocabulary questions); then do the harder ones, guessing on whatever is left when time is up. The important thing is to get credit for those you know you can get right.

Use all of the allotted time. If you finish the Reading Test with extra time, go back and review any questions about which you were in doubt. In order to facilitate this, mark the numbers of those questions on which you were not 100% sure with a diamond-shape so you can quickly identify them.

Know the politics of the test makers.

Insofar as the SAT deals with social themes, it tends to reflect widely held democratic values, especially the idea of progress towards equality and inclusion for all people. Often passages will concern the immigrant experience (the difficulties of assimilating to a new culture or leaving an old one behind), or the role of women in society. The makers of the SAT are careful not to portray any particular social group in a way that is negative or in any way offensive.

Be an efficient bubbler.

Use mnemonic devices to remember chunks of answers as you transfer them to the answer sheet. For example, with a sequence of answers that runs A-B-B-A-D, you might create the phrase "Angry Beatles Bake Apples Daily"

WHAT SKILLS DO I NEED?

General Reading Comprehension Tips

Besides having good test-taking technique, success on the SAT Reading test will require you to efficiently comprehend challenging written passages in English.

Here's how:

Read the blurb. The 'blurb' is the short piece of text preceding the passage. It contains three useful pieces of information:

The title. Sometimes the title will actually state the main idea of the passage or the question that the passage seeks to answer.

Background information. The blurb often contains a short summary or some background knowledge relevant to understanding the passage.

Date of publication. Finally, the blurb will contain the year in which the passage was originally published. An older date of publication — before 1940 or so — means that words might be used in different ways than what you are used to. Also, an old text is likely to involve social situations or make assumptions that are unfamiliar.

Preview. Predict the gist of the passage with a quick skim of the first and last paragraphs as well as of the first sentence of each body paragraph.

Talk to yourself. Maintain a strong 'inner dialogue' to help focus on what you read. Ask questions ("Why is she talking about his example?"), summarize what you've read ("So, she says that inflation is caused by more than just interest rates..."), and be your own coach as you work through the questions.

Use your knowledge of writing structure.

In non-fiction, the main point of a paragraph is often stated in a general way at the beginning or the end.

The main point of the passage as a whole is often stated in the opening and concluding paragraphs.

In fiction, the action tends to proceed towards a climax at the end, a moment in the narrative that reveals theme.

Use your pencil.

Underline important statements.

Box key topics, nouns and subjects.

Circle transitional words and phrases.

Star main ideas or final conclusions.

Skip and return. If something is not making sense, skip to the next paragraph and then return to what you were reading before.

Refer to the questions. The questions might imply certain truths about the passage that can facilitate your comprehension. For example, a question about why two scientists disagree informs you that they do in fact disagree. Likewise, a question about why the author makes use of a sarcastic tone tells you that the passage is meant ironically. Use this to your advantage when the meaning of a passage is unclear to you.

Comprehending Literary Passages

There will be one or two 'literary' passages on the exam – the prose fiction passage at the beginning as well as one of the non-fiction passages.

Literary writing, whether in the form of a story or essay, makes use of metaphor, narrative, and other rhetorical methods to an extent that simple informative writing does not. One of the guiding principles of literary writing is 'show, don't tell.' Such writing appeals to readers' emotions and imaginations at least as much as to their reason. The writer will often make his or her point indirectly, requiring you to infer it from something else.

Although the SAT doesn't require you to know any special terminology, being aware of the following concepts can help you understand this challenging type of writing.

Literary techniques:

1. *Figurative language* occurs when words are used in something other than the literal sense. Literal language just states things as they are. Figurative language tries to express things through comparison or other indirect means.

Some examples of figurative language:

> *Simile*: Comparing two things using 'like' or 'as'

> "Love is like a red, red rose."

> *Metaphor*: Referring to one thing by mentioning another thing

> "All the world's a stage."

> *Allusion*: Referring to something indirectly in order to call it to mind without mentioning it explicitly

> > "The Romeo of his hometown, Alex was never without a love interest."

Hyperbole: Exaggeration to make a point

"If I study any longer, my skull will implode."

Personification: Describing a non-personal thing as if it were a person

"O that your frowns would teach my smiles such skill!"

2. *Imagery* comes from descriptive passages that appeal to the senses in order to add reality to the work.

"The exam room felt like the inside of a meat locker: its walls were silvery white and its air silent, cold, and ripe with the scent of something like freshly butchered mutton."

3. *Point of view* concerns the narrator's relation to what is being expressed

Keep in mind the following aspects of point of view:

In the 'first person' point of view, the narrator writes using the 'I' pronoun and, in the case of a story, is included in the events relayed. This often results in a more personally involved accounting of the events or facts in question.

From the third person point of view, the narrator writes solely using pronouns such as 'he', 'she', and 'they', and assumes a less involved relation to the events relayed.

4. *Tone* has to do with the narrator's attitude toward what is being discussed or the audience to whom the narration is addressed.

Tone can be positive or negative: Is the author offering praise or criticism?

Tone can be formal or informal: Does the author seem very personable and casual in the way she speaks, or does she write in a more proper and emotionally neutral way?

Tone can express many other emotions or attitudes as well; tone can be comic or serious, angry or sarcastic, or just about anything else.

5. A *narrative* is a sequence of interrelated events that tell a story, whether real or fictional. Some passages, such as the fiction excerpt that you will read first on the SAT, will be entirely narrative; others may use a short passage of narrative to make a point.

Some aspects of narrative:

Setting — When and where do the events occur?

Character — Who is involved?

Plot – What happened and how? Understanding plot usually requires you to identify the following:

A premise (problem)

A protagonist (main character)

An antagonist (opposition)

A conflict (struggle)

A climax and resolution (outcome).

Theme (What does it all mean?)

STRATEGIES FOR SPECIFIC QUESTION TYPES

In practicing for the Reading Test, you may come to a point where certain types of questions keep causing trouble for you. Use the following section to get past those tricky questions – or just to gather as much wisdom as possible in your efforts to beat the SAT.

1. Vocabulary Questions

SAT Vocabulary questions ask you what a given word or phrase means as it is used in the passage.

Here's what they usually look like:

As used in line 12, "square" most nearly means

(A) level.

(B) adjacent.

(C) fair.

(D) unfashionable.

Tips for vocabulary questions:

> Usually at least two of the answer choices are correct definitions of the word, although not necessarily the definition used in this context. Remember, words often have more than one meaning.

> Look for specific clues in the sentence that will help determine what the word or phrase means. Consider important words in the sentence, such as 'however', 'but', or 'nevertheless', which might affect the meaning of the word.

> If necessary, look beyond the sentence for clues. Read the sentence before, the sentence after, or even the whole paragraph.

2. Content Questions

This is the most straightforward type of question; you are simply asked to report what the passage says.

> Here's an example of a typical content question:

> The passage indicates that increased computer literacy

(A) has no measurable effect on student achievement.

(B) correlates to family income.

(C) correlates to a decline in other types of literacy.

(D) makes people happier, smarter, and richer.

Tips:

Preview the questions before you read the passage in order to take note of any questions like this one, which don't have specific line references.

Remember: the order of the questions roughly follows the order of the text. For example, if a question is halfway through the series of questions, look for that information halfway through the text.

When in doubt, choose the answer that is conceptually closest to the main idea of the passage. Although not all content questions have to do with the main idea directly, the SAT stays pretty close to the main idea.

Stumped? Sometimes a content question will be followed by an evidence question asking you which quotations from the passage best support the answer to the content question. (See below for more on evidence questions). If you are unsure about the answer to a content question, you can use the answer choices for the evidence question to help locate the answer to the content question.

3. Evidence Questions

Evidence questions ask you to identify the portion of the passage that provides support for a statement.

An evidence question is usually preceded by a content question to which it refers.

For example:

> Which choice provides the best evidence for the answer to the previous question?
>
> (A)   Lines 4-5 ("The dog... happiness")
>
> (B)   Lines 7-9 ("However... America")
>
> (C)   Lines 23-29 ("Students... others")
>
> (D)   Lines 31-40 ("Friendship... success")

Tips:

Reading all the different answer choices and figuring out which quotation is relevant to answering the question can be time consuming, so here are two ways to speed up that process:

(1) Pay attention to the partial quotations in the answer choices; sometimes these words can clue you in to what the relevant evidence might be.

(2) Consider the order of the question within the sequence of questions. An earlier question usually refers to an earlier portion of the passage, and a later question usually refers to a later portion of the passage.

4. Function Questions

Function questions ask you about why the author employs some technique, example, or otherwise about the effect of some aspect of the passage.

Here's an example:

The author most likely uses the quotations in lines 7-11 in order to

(A) establish the veracity of a statement.

(B) challenge an accepted opinion.

(C) call attention to an unstated assumption.

(D) question an accepted authority.

Tips:

First, try finding the answer by examining the immediate context of the item, such as what comes right before and right after.

If that doesn't work, take into consideration the larger structure and purpose of the passage. Try to imagine the whole passage without the item, and ask what difference its absence would make.

If the item in question is a paragraph, then remember what you know about paragraph structure: in most non-fiction writing, the first sentence or two of a paragraph will give you important clues to the function of the paragraph within the passage as a whole. Be especially on the lookout for transitional words and phrases as well as a statement of the paragraph's main idea.

5. Sequence Questions

Sequence questions ask about the organization of the passage or the order of events described in the passage.

Here's an example:

> Over the course of the passage, the focus shifts from
>
> (A) early American history to present day events.
>
> (B) the presentation of an argument to evidence for it.

(C) a general idea to examples of the general idea.

(D) a general idea to personal testimony in support of the idea.

Tips:

Remember: the first sentence or two in a paragraph will often state the main idea of that paragraph. Using this knowledge, you can sometimes quickly skim the passage to determine its developmental structure.

Pay attention to the use of logically significant transitional words and phrases in the passage, such as 'therefore', 'on the contrary', or 'on the other hand.' These words can give you clues to identify important developments in the text.

If you are using the backsolving technique discussed above, seeing this question in your preview should remind you to take careful note of how the passage develops as you read.

6. Logic & Inference Questions

Logic & Inference questions ask about logical relationships in the passage. For example, they may ask about:

- Assumptions

- Implications

- Potential contradictions

Here is one example of this type of question:

Which of the following choices would contradict the author's point of view?

(A) Weight loss can be achieved by a high protein, low carbohydrate diet.

(B) Exercise alone is sufficient to maintain weight loss.

(C) The amount of fat in one's diet is irrelevant to weight loss.

(D) Weight loss is always just a matter of the differential between caloric intake and caloric use.

And here's another:

An unstated assumption made in the argument expressed in lines 34-41 is

(A) only certain dog breeds make for good companions.

(B) no cats are capable of loyalty.

(C) the ideal pet is relative to the owner's lifestyle.

(D) all pet owners desire pets for the sake of companionship.

Tips:

Following the tips for active reading, use your pencil to circle words or phrases that express reasoning. Two important types of such words are:

Premise indicator words -- used to present a premise (a reason) in support of a conclusion — e.g., since, *because, for, in that, given that, for the reason that, may be inferred from.*

Conclusion indicator words -- used to present the conclusion (the main point) of an argument — e.g., *therefore, accordingly, entails that, hence, thus, consequently, so, it follows that, as a result.*

If you are unable to answer a Logic & Inference question right away, try doing some of the other questions in order to clarify your overall understanding of the passage.

Consider every word carefully. Answers go wrong based upon the slightest wording. Remember, an answer that is partly right and partly wrong is just plain wrong as far as the test goes. 99% right is 100% wrong!

7. Main Idea Questions

This type of question will ask about the 'main idea', 'main point', 'central claim', or 'conclusion' of the passage.

For example:

Which choice best summarizes the passage?

(A) The modern appreciation of wilderness would have been inconceivable before Romanticism.

(B) Outdoor activities provide a welcome relief from the pressures of industrial society.

(C) Many outdoor activities function as forms of conspicuous consumption.

(D) The psychological benefits of wilderness-based recreation show that modern living conditions are not conducive to personal well being.

Here are some tips for Main Idea questions:

Save them for last. Solving the more detail-oriented questions first will help you answer these more general questions.

Look for a statement of the main idea at the beginning of the passage or at the end of the passage. Check the blurb; sometimes the title of the passage will tell you the main idea or at least help you to figure out what it is.

Look out for the three types of main idea answer traps:

(1) Too specific

(2) Too general

(3)   Something mentioned in the passage but not the main idea

Remember, the main idea will often not be stated explicitly, and so you will have to infer it. Although this is especially true of the fiction and literary passages, it can apply to the other passages as well.

8. Tone Questions

Tone questions are relatively rare on the SAT, but you will encounter a few. Tone concerns authors' attitudes towards their subject or audience.

Here's an example:

The author's attitude toward Jerry Garcia is best described as

(A)   Mocking.

(B)   Indifferent.

(C)   Open-minded.

(D)   Appreciative.

Tips:

Here are three questions you can ask to help determine the tone of a passage:

(1)   Is it subjective or objective? In a subjective piece, the author's opinions or emotions will come through. In an objective piece, such as what one might read in an encyclopedia,

a textbook, or news reporting, the author remains entirely neutral in his or her presentation.

(2)　If it is subjective, determine whether the tone is negative or positive. Does the author express an opinion that is especially critical of the subject matter, or does the author express a more upbeat view?

(3)　Finally, ask whether there are any other defining aspects to the tone of the passage? Is it humorous, sarcastic, angry, playful, reverential, or anything else?

The answers to tone questions typically proceed in order from negative to positive, or from positive to negative. This can be especially helpful if you do not know some of the vocabulary. For example, if you didn't know the meaning of the word 'indifferent' in the question above, you could infer that it means something between 'mocking' and 'open-minded.'

9. Graphics Questions

In two of the SAT Reading sections you will encounter a few questions that ask you to read, interpret, and apply data expressed in graphs, charts or tables.

Sometimes these questions will focus entirely on the graph.

Here's an example:

In the graph, which measurement represents the average rainfall for the month of August in the city of New York in the 1990s?

(A) 106 millimeters

(B) 111 millimeters

(C) 120 millimeters

(D) 135 millimeters

Other times, the question will ask you to relate the information in the graph to the passage.

For example:

Which concept is supported by the passage and the information in the graph?

(A) Since the beginning of the 20th century New York has seen a decrease in average August rainfall.

(B) Since the beginning of the 20th century, New York has seen an increase in average August rainfall.

(C) Changes in August rainfall for New York have matched meteorologists' predictions.

(D) Changes in August rainfall for New York have contradicted meteorologists' predictions.

Tips for graphic questions:

Remember, the graphics stand on their own and don't require you to refer to the text in order to make sense of them.

If some aspect of the data represented seems extreme or significant in some way, take note, since frequently the question will have to do with this information.

If you are unsure of how to answer a graphics question, use the process of elimination: work through each answer choice, checking the data in the graph and crossing out wrong answers.

Graph questions that also refer to the passage require two steps. The first is to interpret the data in the graph (again, take note of whatever stands out as being important or interesting), and the second is to consider what the passage says in this regard. Since the questions often stay close to the main idea, the main idea of the passage can sometimes help you to understand how the passage relates to the information in the graph.

10. Paired Passages

One of the five reading sections on the reading test will involve two passages dealing with closely related topics.

Roughly one third of the questions will refer to the first passage, one third to the second, and one third to both.

The main hazard for the paired passages comes from confusing the meanings of the passages. This problem can be avoided by summarizing the main point of each passage when you have finished reading it. You can do this by underlining a key part of the text, or, better yet, writing out the idea.

Method for answering paired passages:

> Read Passage One, answer questions that refer to it, then clearly summarize main idea.
>
> Read Passage Two, answer questions that refer to it, then clearly summarize main idea.
>
> Answer questions that refer to both passages.

HOW DO I PREPARE FOR THE READING TEST?

Now that you know what's necessary for succeeding on the SAT Reading Test, all that's left to do is prepare.

Here's how:

Follow the general guidelines in the section of this book called How to Prepare for the SAT.

If you have three months or more:

- Take regular practice tests, although take them less frequently than you would in the three months leading up to the test -- perhaps once a week.

- Become an SAT expert: analyze old practice tests and come up with your own theories about how the SAT works.

- If vocabulary turns out to be a problem in your practice, consider doing vocab-building work. This work can also help with the Essay Test.

- Read lots of quality writing, such as what you might find in the *New Yorker*, the *Atlantic*, the *New York Times*, and the *Economist*. Focus on whatever your weaknesses are:

If you are missing a lot of fiction or literary passages, read novels and short stories.

If older passages stump you, read 19th century literature (e.g., Charles Dickens, Jane Austin, Edgar Allen Poe, Mark Twain).

If you find the science passages hard, read good popular science writing, such as that found in magazines like *Scientific American, Discover, and National Geographic.*

If you have less than three months until the test:

- Work through this chapter and make sure you thoroughly understand all the methods, tips, and information.

- Take at least 2 to 3 practice tests per week.

- Always take note of the questions you are missing, and use this guide to help with those that are giving you problems.

- If you hit a plateau, hire a qualified tutor.

2.
The Writing and Language Section

The Writing and Language Test follows the Reading Test and is the second section you will take on the SAT.

The questions deal with 4 different passages that need editing – one each from social studies, humanities, science, and career-related topics.

These passages contain errors in development and organization, economy and precision of expression, word choice, grammar, and punctuation.

The test allows you 35 minutes to answer 44 questions - an average of 11 minutes per passage.

Some of the questions refer to tables or graphics that accompany the reading.

Your score on the Writing and Language Test will be combined with your score on the Reading Test for a total Reading and Writing score of 200-800. This will make up half of your final score out of 1600.

WHAT METHOD SHOULD I USE?

The more you practice for the SAT, the more you will perfect your own style of test taking. Here is a general plan of attack to get you started:

(1) Read each passage for comprehension, since skipping will put you at risk for misunderstanding some questions.

(2) For each question, try to determine the solution *before* looking at the answers.

(3) If a question refers to a more general portion of the passage, such as a paragraph, be sure to consider the question relative to that *entire* segment

(4) Eliminate wrong answers.

(5) Don't shy away from the NO CHANGE option; it comes up as much as anything else.

(6) If you are stumped by a question, circle the number in order to return to it later.

(7) Check the time after the second passage; you should have at least 18 minutes left.

(8) When you complete the last question of each section, go back to any unanswered questions you have circled.

(9) Answer *every* question; if you don't know an answer, eliminate what you can, and guess.

(10) As you complete each passage, bubble your answers on the answer sheet using mnemonic devices to help you transfer them. (For example: A-B-C-B-C = "Angry Beasts Cause Big Crashes")

WHAT SKILLS DO I NEED?

Of course, to do well on the Writing and Language test you will also need to understand some basic rules of English grammar, usage, expression, and punctuation. While you probably already know a lot, the following section, which focuses on the errors most common to the SAT, will help you sharpen your skills.

Here are some rules of thumb:

Grammar, Usage, and Expression

1. Avoid sentence fragments:

A complete sentence contains a subject, a predicate, and expresses a complete thought.

> Incorrect: "The snowflakes began to dot my windshield. Ashes from a distant fire."

Correct: "Like ashes from a distant fire, the snowflakes dotted my windshield."

2. Make sure to use logically appropriate words when linking a dependent clause to an independent clause:

Incorrect: "<u>Since</u> he was class valedictorian, he really knew nothing about literature, history, or philosophy"

Correct: "<u>Although</u> he was class valedictorian, he really knew nothing about literature, history, or philosophy."

3. When using the first part of a correlative conjunction, make sure to use the second part as well:

Some common correlative conjunctions: *neither/nor, either/or, both/and, not only/but, between/and, whether/or, such/that.*

Incorrect: "I find it very hard to choose between apple pie <u>or</u> chocolate cake."

Correct: "I find it very hard to choose between apple pie and chocolate cake."

4. Avoid comma splices and other run-ons:

A *run-on sentence* is two independent clauses put together with no punctuation or with a comma (in which case it is called a *comma splice*).

An *independent clause* is a complete sentence that can stand on its own.

Incorrect: "That was my favorite game of the <u>year, the</u> Mariners hit 8 home runs."

Correct: "That was my favorite game of the year; the Mariners hit 8 home runs."

The first sentence is incorrect because it links two independent clauses with a comma.

5. Observe parallel structure:

Parallel structure involves expressing things in similar patterns of words to show equality of importance, as in lists or comparisons.

Incorrect: "My morning workout involves running, weightlifting, and <u>to stretch</u>."

Correct: "My morning workout involves running, weightlifting, and <u>stretching</u>."

The first sentence is incorrect because the first two members of the list are gerunds and the third is an infinitive.

6. Place modifiers next to what they are intended to modify:

A *modifier* is a word, phrase, or clause that describes or qualifies some other part of the sentence.

Incorrect: "<u>Drinking my tea at sunset, the mountain</u> looked like a woman lying on her side."

Correct: "Drinking my tea at sunset, <u>I thought</u> the mountain looked like a woman lying on her side."

The first sentence is incorrect because the introductory phrase is placed next to a noun it is not intended to modify.

6. Stay consistent in verb tense within sentences and among consecutive sentences dealing with the same subject:

> Incorrect: "After I had gone to the grocery store, I went to the bank, where I <u>see</u> a guy <u>I know</u> from some years ago."

> Correct: "After I had gone to the grocery store, I went the bank, where I saw a guy I knew from some years ago."

The first sentence is incorrect because it shifts to the present tense after having established that the sentence is in the past tense.

7. Stay consistent in the person and number of pronouns within sentences and among related sentences:

> Incorrect: "Our company is the best in the business; you can really trust <u>them</u> to get the job done."

> Correct: "Our company is the best in the business; you can really trust us to get the job done."

8. Make sure every pronoun has a clear reference:

> Incorrect: "My dog bit my neighbor's wife because <u>she</u> has a bad temper."

> Correct: "My dog bit my neighbor's wife because my dog has a bad temper."

9. Make sure pronouns and nouns agree with their antecedents in person and number:

The *antecedent* of a pronoun is the noun it stands in for.

Pronouns:

> Incorrect: "In the World Cup, the United States has a good chance; they should make it to the second round at least."

> Correct: In the World Cup, the United States has a good chance; it should make it to the second round at least.

Nouns:

> Incorrect: "All of my classmates want to be a lawyer after they graduate."

> Correct: "All of my classmates want to be lawyers after they graduate."

10. Make sure verbs match with their subjects in person and number:

A few rules to remember here:

Compound subjects joined by *and* are plural.

> Incorrect: "Singing and playing piano is my favorite pastime."

> Correct: "Singing and playing piano are my favorite pastimes."

Compound subjects joined by *or* or *nor* follow the subject closest to the verb.

> Incorrect: Either running or swimming are a great way to build cardio."

> Correct: Either running or swimming is a great way to build cardio."

When a phrase comes between subject and verb, be careful not to confuse the actual subject with the word that comes immediately before the verb.

> Incorrect: Each of the chickens were producing three eggs a day.

> Correct: Each of the chickens was producing three eggs a day.

11. Look out for frequently confused words:

Here are some especially common ones:

> Its/it's: *Its* is possessive and *it's* is a contraction of it and is.

> Their/ they're/there: *Their* is possessive, *they're* is a contraction of they and are, and *there* is an adverb indicating a specific place or that something exists.

> Than/then: *Than* introduces a comparison, *then* can express either order in time or logical consequence.

> Who/which/that: *Who* and sometimes *that* refer to people; which only refers to things.

Accept/except: *Accept* means to receive with approval; *except* expresses exclusion.

Affect, effect: Usually, *affect* is a verb meaning to influence, while *effect* is a noun denoting a thing influenced.

Conscience/ conscious: *Conscience* refers to a person's sense of moral right and wrong; *conscious* means awake or aware.

Who/ whom: *Whom* is a relative pronoun that refers to the *object* of a verb or pronoun; *who* names the *subject* of a clause.

> Tip: Ask yourself whether the pronoun is doing something; if it is, then you should use *who*.

>> Incorrect: I don't just take advice from anyone <u>whom</u> gives it.

>> Incorrect: We were disappointed by the guitarist <u>who</u> we hired for our wedding.

12. When making comparisons, make sure the things compared are related according to the appropriate kind:

> Incorrect: "My fantasy football team is better than <u>John</u>."

> Correct: "My fantasy football team is better than <u>John's team</u>."

13. Avoid vague language:

> Incorrect: "He's an old-fashioned guy who's into cars, tools <u>and stuff</u>."

14. Avoid redundancies and wordiness:

Redundancy:

> Incorrect: "The meeting will commence at 8 AM <u>in the morning</u>."

Wordiness:

> Incorrect: "When the summer after this one eventually comes, we will proceed to travel to Argentina."

> Correct: "Next summer, we will travel to Argentina."

15. Maintain consistent and appropriate style and tone:

> Incorrect: "The investigators eventually concluded that the anomalies in the data were not accidents but rather the result of deliberate misrepresentation... which just goes to show: when it's time to stack up the benjamins, even a Nobel laureate can go gangster on you."

Punctuation

1. Don't end an indirect question with a question mark:

> Incorrect: "Thelma asked me if I would like to take a little drive out West<u>?</u>"

Correct: "Thelma asked me if I would like to take a little drive out West."

2. Use commas correctly:

Use commas to set off non-essential information from the main clause of the sentence.

"My youngest child, a champion eater since infancy, devoured two frozen pizzas and a half gallon of ice cream."

Use commas to separate items in a series.

"According to Chuck Klosterman, a great writer must be clear, interesting, and entertaining."

Use commas to set off geographical names and personal titles.

"The greater metropolitan area of Lagos, Nigeria, is home to more than twenty million people."

Use commas before quotations.

It was Emerson who said, "The earth laughs in flowers."

Use commas to separate two or more adjectives that refer to the same noun.

"When I grow up I want to be a dirty, rotten, stinking, filthy, rich person."

Don't use commas to separate an adjective from a noun it describes.

Incorrect: "The pointed, towering, peak in the Alps looked exactly like an arrowhead."

3. Use semicolons to join two independent clauses when there is need for a pause longer than a comma but shorter than a period.

"One does not belong to a country; one belongs to a language. It is words, not borders, that define the boundaries of the self."

4. Use colons at the end of sentences that introduce lists, quotations, explanations, or examples:

Tip#1: The colon functions much like an equals sign: what comes after is roughly equivalent to what comes before.

Tip#2: Make sure that the sentence before the colon is an independent clause.

"If you want to understand jazz saxophone, there are just three names you need to know: Coleman Hawkins, Charlie Parker, and John Coltrane"

5. Use a single dash following an independent clause in exactly the same way you would use a colon.

6. Use a pair of dashes in the same way you would use a pair of parentheses (or a pair of commas)—to set off nonessential information from the main clause of the sentence.

Tip: If you remove what is between the pair of dashes (or parentheses or commas), the remaining sentence should still be an independent clause.

> "The smaller of my two dogs — blissfully unaware of his diminutive stature — is the louder and more aggressive."

7. Form the possessive of a singular noun by adding an apostrophe and *s*, whether or not the noun ends in *s*.

> "Descartes's clever arguments continue to challenge beginning philosophy students 400 years later."

8. Form the possessive of a plural noun by adding only an apostrophe when the noun ends in *s* and adding *'s* when the noun ends in a letter other than *s*.

> "Scholars' interpretations of Shakespeare's writings have varied widely over the centuries."

Strategies for Specific Question Types

In practicing for the Writing and Language test, you may come to a point where certain types of questions keep causing trouble for you. Use the following section to get past those tricky questions – or just to gather as much wisdom as possible in your efforts to beat the SAT.

1. Word Choice Questions

In word choice questions you are asked to choose the word that fits best in the context.

Here are some tips:

> Underline the word in the passage, and look for clues in the surrounding text to help infer the meaning of that space in the sentence.

> If you don't recognize a word, look for any roots or prefixes you might know. You can also try pronouncing the word aloud or using it in a sentence.

> If you are stumped as to the specific meaning of a word, try to guess whether it has a positive or negative connotation.

> If two of the answer choices mean the same thing, or very nearly the same thing, eliminate them (since the SAT strives to avoid disputable answers).

> Make sure to choose an answer that is consistent in tone and style with the context.

2. Transition Questions

In this type of question, you will be asked to choose the transitional word or phrase — such as "however," "moreover," or "on the other hand" — that best suits the context.

Here's how to do it:

> Read as much before and after as necessary to determine the logical relationship the transition should express.
>
> Look for other transitional words and phrases in the text to help you understand the logical flow of the text.
>
> As above, eliminate choices that express the same logical relationship, since none of these are be the right answer.

3. Logical Organization Questions

An example of this type of question:

> To make this paragraph most logical, sentence 4 should be placed
>
> (A) where it now.
>
> (B) after sentence 2.
>
> (C) after sentence 4.
>
> (D) after sentence 5.

Here's a method that can help:

> Step One: Carefully read the paragraph from the beginning and look for anything that sounds out of order (such as an allusion to something that has not been mentioned yet).
>
> Step Two: When you have located this disorder, determine where before this

point in the paragraph the sentence in the question should be placed.

Step Three: Plug the sentence in and read through to see if everything now makes sense.

Step Four: If you don't see anything out of order, choose option A), "where it is now."

4. Deletion/Addition Questions

This question will ask you whether or not a sentence – or part of a sentence -- should be deleted or added, as well as why or why not.

It looks like this:

At this point, the writer is considering adding the following sentence.

"Rose made the lemonade with lemons she picked from her family's citrus grove."

Should the writer make this addition here?

(A) Yes, because it helps the reader to understand Rose's background.

(B) Yes, because it provides a helpful example to support a generalization about Rose's character.

(C) No, because it is irrelevant and distracts from the main point of the passage.

(D)   No, because it contradicts some-
      thing stated earlier in tee text.

When you make this choice, consider the
following:

Relevance: Does the item in question fit with the main point of the
paragraph?

Redundancy: Does the item in question merely repeat information mentioned earlier?

Coherence: Does the item in question
fit with the logical and stylistic flow of
sentences before and after?

5. Sentence Combining Questions

In this type of question you will be asked
which option most effectively combines the
two sentences at the underlined portion.

Some tips:

Make sure the answer you choose
contains all the info expressed in the
two sentences.

Make sure the answer you choose is
a well-composed, grammatically correct sentence.

When in doubt, choose the answer that
is clearest and most concise.

6. Graphics Questions

This type of question asks you to interpret or otherwise apply data from a graphic to the text.

For example:

> "Which choice accurately and effectively represents the info in the graph...?"

Here's how to do it:

> Don't worry about the data until you come to a question that references a graphic.

> Quickly look over the graphic, noting what information it expresses, along with any especially important aspects of the data.

> Work through the answers, checking the graph as you go and eliminating options that don't work.

7. Conceptual and Stylistic Cohesion Questions

This type of question concerns issues of relevance, logical support, organization, and consistency of style and tone.

Such questions might take the following forms, or many others:

> "Which choice best completes the description...?"

"Which choice provides information that best supports the claim made by this/previous sentence...?

"Which choice provides the most relevant detail...?"

"Which choice most closely matches the stylistic pattern established earlier in the sentence...?"

"Over the course of the passage, the focus shifts from..."

Tips:

Make sure you read the passage for comprehension, since this whole class of questions requires that you are following the text closely.

Look for the *best* answer. Beware of answers that seem okay but not ideal.

Look out for anything that strays from the main idea of each paragraph.

If you are having trouble interpreting the meaning of part of the passage, such a paragraph, consider the larger context, especially the main idea. If you are unclear on the main idea of the passage, look at the title.

Look at the beginning or end of a paragraph — often the first or last sentence — to help determine its main idea.

Use transitional words and phrases to help follow the organizational structure of the essay.

Avoid shifts in style from *formal* to *informal*, as well as shifts in tone from *objective* to *subjective*, *positive* to *negative*, *serious* to *humorous*, or in any other ways that would be inconsistent.

HOW DO I PREPARE FOR THE WRITING AND LANGUAGE TEST?

Now that you know what's necessary for succeeding on the SAT Writing and Language Test, all that's left to do is prepare.

Here's how:

Follow the general guidelines in the section of this book called How to Prepare for the SAT.

If you have three months or more:

Take regular practice tests. Aim for one a week until you have less than three months to go until your test.

Learn more about grammar, usage, expression and punctuation by reading up on areas of confusion and doing practice drills. An old-fashioned grammar workbook can be helpful for this purpose, and there are many excellent resources online.

Become an SAT expert: analyze old practice tests and come up with your own theories about the kinds of questions and issues the SAT focuses on.

If you have less than three months until the test:

Work through this chapter and make sure you thoroughly understand all the principles of grammar, usage, expression and punctuation.

Take at least 2 to 3 practice tests per week.

Always take note of the questions you are missing, and use this guide to help with those that are giving you problems.

If you hit a plateau, hire a qualified tutor.

3.
The Math Section

The SAT Math Test follows the Writing and Language Test and makes up the third and fourth sections on the SAT. While the underlying content should be familiar, what makes the SAT Math Test so challenging is the *way* the problems are presented, often with wording that is intended to throw you off.

To do well on the SAT Math Test, you will need to:

    (1)   *identify what the questions are asking*

    (2)   *find the right answers as quickly as possible.*

The SAT Math Test is made up of two sections:

- The No Calculator Section with 20 questions

- The Calculator Section with 38 questions.

Below is a table with the time limits for each section, *though you should aim to spend 60-75 seconds per problem.*

Section	Time Limit	# of Questions
No Calculator Section	25 minutes	20 questions
Calculator Section	55 minutes	38 questions

The College Board has broken up the math you'll need into four content areas.

Content Area	Math Topics
Heart of Algebra (19 questions, 33%)	*Solving linear equations, inequalities, and systems of linear equations; using linear equations and inequalities to represent relationships*
Problem Solving & Data Analysis (17 questions, 29%)	*Modeling of real-world problems; ratios, rates and proportional relationships; interpretation of graphs and data tables; basic statistics (probability, measures of central tendency)*
Passport to Advanced Math (16 questions, 28%)	*Analyzing, manipulating, and solving quadratic and other nonlinear equations; working with exponents, radicals, polynomials, and quadratic functions*
Additional Topics in Math (6 questions, 10%)	*Applying various geometric and trigonometric concepts related to lines, angles, triangles and circles; finding area and volume of common shapes and objects*

Even though there is a section that allows the use of a calculator, it is possible to solve almost every problem on the test without one. Only use the calculator when it will help you solve a problem more quickly and more accurately. *Tip: bring a calculator you are used to using to the test.*

There are 13 questions that are not multiple choice, which are referred to as *grid-ins*. There are eight grid-in problems at the end of the Calculator Section and five grid-ins at the end of the No Calculator Section.

On these problems, it is possible for there to be more than one right answer, but you should grid-in *only one answer* for every problem. Also, the answers on these problems will *always* be positive and less than 9999. Below are a some examples of how to fill in the answers for a gridded-response question:

There are also a few problems that are referred to as *extended thinking* problems, where multiple questions are asked about the same given scenario or data set. Usually just two questions are asked on these types of problems, and they are most likely to appear on the Calculator section.

At the beginning of each math section, there is a reference page that contains some useful facts and formulas for common two- and three-dimensional shapes. There is a replica of the reference page in the last section of this chapter. A list of essential formulas and facts not on the reference page are listed at the end of this chapter.

WHAT SKILLS DO I NEED?

Don't overcomplicate things. The problems are designed to obscure the fact that the underlying math is fairly basic. SAT Math is high school math. Virtually all the problems on the SAT Math Test will be rooted in concepts and skills that you have learned in school.

Pace Yourself. Be mindful of the time and work efficiently, without causing yourself to feel unnecessary stress, which will only hinder your ability to solve problems quickly and accurately. The more you practice, the more comfortable and confident you will be on test day.

Skipping is OK. It is much better to guess on some questions and put in your best effort on the rest than it is to put in less effort on everything. If you cannot make sense of a problem after 30 seconds, either make a smart guess on it or use an alternative strategy.

Eliminate obviously wrong choices. Eliminate one or two answer choices if you can. There is usually at least one option that is there because it is the result of some common error or miscalculation. Identifying and eliminating these options will raise your chances of guessing correctly to either 33 or 50%. Here is an example:

> Over the past 12 months, the number of subscribers to the YouTube channel, UnspeakableGaming, has increased by 75%. If the channel currently has Y subscribers, how many did it have 12 months ago?
>
> (C) 0.57Y
>
> (D) 0.75Y
>
> (E) 1.33Y
>
> (F) 1.75Y
>
> *Solution*: Since the number of subscribers has increased, the number of subscribers 12 months ago must be *less* than the current number, Y. Answers (C) and (D) would be *greater*, so they can be eliminated. The correct answer is (A).

Answer everything. There are no penalties for wrong answers, so be sure you have bubbled in an answer for every multiple choice question, even if it is a guess. You may even want to skip the last few multiple choice questions so that you can attempt the first few grid-ins, which are likely going to be less difficult.

Read carefully. In order to have the best chance of finding the right answer, you need to be certain of what the task is and what the relevant information is. So, read carefully, strategize quickly, and then work methodically through the problem.

Identify keywords. Once you know what the task is, you need to figure out how to accomplish that task. Below is a table of some of the common keywords and their corresponding translations:

Keywords	Math Translation
is, are, was, equal, as much as, as long as	=
sum, increased by, more than	+
difference, decreased by, less than	−
product, of, times	×
quotient, out of, per, divided by, ratio	÷

Mark it up. The test booklet is yours. *Write in it!* Circle or underline keywords, draw pictures, set up equations, make lists, cross out wrong answers, write whatever will help you find the right answer as quickly as possible. Doing mental math is risky during high-pressure tests, so writing things down will also help guard against careless mistakes.

Simplify, simplify, simplify. If fractions are not in lowest terms, reduce them. If a common factor can be factored out on both sides of an equation, divide both sides by it to get rid of it. If like terms can be combined, combine them. If there are parentheses, distribute. You get the idea. Here is an example of how to use this tip:

> In the popular video game, *Minecraft*, materials and tools can be used to make other materials and tools. For example, wood planks, *p*, can be used to make sticks, *s*, and wood planks can be combined with sticks to make wood pickaxes, *a*. The following equations show the relationships between these materials and items:

$$2p = 4s$$

$$2s + 3p = a$$

What does *a* equal in terms of *p*?

(A) $3.5p$

(B) $4p$

(C) $5p$

(D) $6p$

Solution: The first equation can be simplified to $p = 2s$, and $2s$ happens to be the first term in the second equation. You can substitute p for $2s$ in the second equation and then combine like terms: $(p) + 3p = 4p$. The answer is choice (B).

Don't do more than you have to. Remember that the SAT Math Test is mostly a multiple choice test. The right answer is already there on the page, and there are often faster ways to choose the right answer than actually solving for it like you would in school. The test writers know this, and they expect you to use shortcuts and strategies like the ones in this book.

WHAT METHOD SHOULD I USE?

Even though the SAT Math Test covers a wide range of concepts and skills, there are a handful of attack strategies you can use depending on what the question is asking, what information is given, and what the answer choices are.

Regardless of what strategy you use, working through a problem will involve four fundamental steps:

(1) Read the question: *What do these words on the page mean?*

(2) Identify the task: *What are you being asked to do?*

(3) Identify the relevant information: *What information is given and how will you use it?*

(4) Work through the problem and find the answer!

Mark things up as you read, circling or underlining keywords, numbers, and the sentence that tells you what the task is (Ex. "...what is the value of x?" or "what is the greatest integer?").

For most problems, the information in the prompt (or figure or graph or table) will be what you use to find the right answer. At other times, you can *plug in your own numbers*. Using the answer choices themselves and *backsolving* is another great strategy to use for certain types of problems. Quickly survey the answer choices as part of your reading of the question.

Method #1: The Natural

This strategy involves reading the prompt, identifying the task, and then solving the problem.

This approach should be familiar to you. This will be most like the way you solve math problems in high school.

If you struggle translating words directly into numbers and symbols, drawing a picture or making a table may help you visualize the problem, especially when it involves geometry, trigonometry, or functions.

When it might be good to use The Natural:

(1) on most problems involving graphs, figures, or data tables

(2) on grid-in problems

(3) when you have to calculate an answer using a formula or theorem.

Here is a good example of a problem you would use this strategy on:

Time (minutes)	Number of fans
0	1,000
30	16,000
60	31,000
90	46,000

Taylor Swift performed in a stadium recently and 1,000 superfans were allowed entry two hours early for a pre-show meet-and-greet. The gates for general admission then opened 90 minutes before showtime. The table above gives the initial number of fans inside the stadium (at time $t = 0$) and tracks how the number of fans increased over the 90-minute period of general admission. Which of the following functions best models the number of fans, $F(t)$, after t minutes?

(A) $F(t) = 1,000 + 30t$

(B) $F(t) = 1,000 + 15,000t$

(C) $F(t) = 1,000 + 500t$

(D) $F(t) = 15,000 + 500t$

Solution: The number of fans increased by 15,000 during each 30-minute time period, and since that is a constant rate of change, this is a linear function. To calculate the rate of change, divide 15,000 fans by 30 minutes, which is 500 fans/minute. So, for every minute, t, that passes, 500 fans entered the stadium, which can be expressed as 500t. There were already 1,000 fans inside the stadium at $t = 0$, so to find the number of fans at any given minute after $t = 0$, add 1,000 to 500t, which would be answer choice (C) $F(t) = 1,000 + 500t$.

Depending on the problem, working through problems in this way, from start to finish, is not always the fastest.

Method #2: Plug In Your Own Numbers

Occasionally, there are problems that appear to be much more difficult than they actually are. This usually happens when there are multiple variables or unknowns in the problem, which can make finding the solution algebraically seem impossible, especially when you should be aiming to spend only 60-75 seconds per problem. Plugging in your own numbers offers a way to avoid doing algebra.

This strategy can often make difficult problems much easier to solve by allowing you to see how relationships expressed by equations or functions play out with actual numbers. It can also help you eliminate answer choices if you must guess.

Start with small numbers like 2, 3 or 4. Avoid picking 0 and 1 because they have weird properties, and avoid large numbers because they would overcomplicate the problem. Keep your numbers simple, and make sure they are consistent with any requirements in the prompt.

When it might be good to plug in your own numbers:

(1) when the question and/or answer choices contain variables

(2) on problems involving percent increases or decreases,

(3) after you translate the words in a problem into a mathematical ex-

pression or equation (assigning variables, as needed).

Below is an example of a problem you could use this strategy on:

If x is equal to y divided by z, which of the following expressions would be equal to y multiplied by z?

(A) $\frac{xy}{z}$

(B) $\frac{x}{z}$

(C) $\frac{xz}{y}$

(D) xz^2

Solution: First, translate the words into an equation: $x = \frac{y}{z}$. Then, assign some easy numbers to the variables that satisfy that equation. Here are three numbers that work:

$$x = 3, \ y = 6, \ z = 2$$

We know these work because $3 = \frac{6}{2}$. Next, since you are asked to see what expression is equal to $y \times z$, evaluate $y \times z$ using the numbers you picked: (6)(2) = 12. Finally, go through the answer choices, substituting your numbers in for the variables until you get an answer that equals 12, like so:

(A) $\frac{xy}{z} = \frac{(3)(6)}{(2)} = 9 \neq 12$ *Does not work.*

(B) $\frac{x}{z} = \frac{3}{2} \neq 12$ *Does not work.*

(C) $\frac{xz}{y} = \frac{(3)(2)}{(6)} = 1 \neq 12$ *Does not work.*

(D) $xz^2 = (3)(2)^2 = 12$ *Woohoo!*

> You may need to choose multiple numbers to test the answers because the numbers you chose may work for more than one answer choice.

Method #3: Backsolving

Just like Method #2, this is a great approach to use when you are facing a difficult problem that involves variables. To use it, you simply plug the answer choices into an equation that is either given in the prompt or generated by you after translating the scenario into an equation.

> Backsolving is an easy way to find the right answer without having to do a lot of algebra. Also, the numbers and options to try are right there on the page!

Numerical answer choices are usually arranged from least to greatest (Ex. (A) 1 (B) 10 (C) 100 (D) 1,000), so you should start in the middle with answer choice B or C. You should then be able to determine if you need to go lower or higher if your first choice did not work. If you start in the middle and also eliminate any obviously wrong answers, then you will save a lot of time when using this strategy.

When it might be good to use this strategy:

(1) on multiple choice problems with answer choices that are numbers

(2) after you have translated the words in a prompt into a mathematical expression or equation (assigning variables, if necessary)

(3) you want to check the answer that you arrived at algebraically

(4) you are stuck and don't know what else to do.

See the example below:

The genetically resurrected *Tyrannosaurus Rex* was quite full Saturday evening after feasting on one-sixth of the human safety inspectors who had arrived at the dinosaur park earlier that day. The *T. Rex* rested on Sunday but then continued his hunt on Monday, eating two more humans and then three on Tuesday. If there were 15 survivors remaining in the park on Wednesday, how many humans were there on Saturday before the *T. Rex* began his multi-day feast?

(A) 18

(B) 20

(C) 24

(D) 36

Solution: Review what you know first: 15 humans remain on Wednesday, 3 were eaten on Tuesday, 2 were eaten on Monday, and one-sixth of the initial number were eaten on Saturday. If you assign a variable for the initial number of humans, like x, here is the equation you will use when backsolving:

$$x - 3 - 2 - \frac{1}{6}x = 15$$

Solving for x is obviously an option but it would take multiple steps and you could probably find the right answer more quickly by backsolving and doing the calculations in your head. Start with (B) and work backwards:

$$20 - 3 - 2 - \frac{1}{6}(20) = ?...$$

20 is not evenly divisible by 6 so that cannot be the correct choice.

Answer (A) can be thrown out since 18 people would not be a large enough number to start out with. Try (C) next:

$$24 - 3 - 2 - \frac{1}{6}(24) = 24 - 3 - 2 - 4 = 15$$

Bingo! (C) is the right answer since 15 visitors were left after subtracting the *T. Rex*'s meals.

Since you are potentially trying out multiple choices before landing on the right answer, this approach can take some time. Also, as you noticed with this problem, it is rarely so simple as just plugging in the answers, and you will likely need to do some work beforehand, like generating an equation or expression from the prompt or simplifying an equation that was given.

TIPS FOR SPECIFIC QUESTION TYPES

The previous section described a few general attack strategies to use depending on what the task is and what the answer choices look like.

This section will walk you through how to apply those strategies to the different question types that will appear on the test.

Word Problems

Word problems are one of the most common question types on the SAT Math Test.

Below is an example word problem, and your first steps will be to *read the prompt and identify the information you will need to solve the problem*, including any keywords, numbers, rates, and units.

> Ariana Grande is five feet tall and her ponytail is currently 36 inches long. Her hair grows 0.5 inches per month with proper care and conditioning. Based on this information, how many years will it take for her ponytail to be as long as she is tall?
>
> (A) 2
>
> (B) 4
>
> (C) 12
>
> (D) 16

Aside from identifying the task during your first reading, you should *be an active reader and underline the key pieces of information.* Here is what the prompt should look like after you read it:

> Ariana Grande is <u>five feet tall</u> and her ponytail is currently <u>36 inches long</u>. Her hair <u>grows 0.5 inches per month</u> with proper care and conditioning. Based on this information, <u>how many years will it take for her ponytail to be as long as she is tall?</u>

Underlined are the numbers and their units as well as the question that reveals the task.

Your next step will be to *determine how the given pieces of information are related* and *how you will use that information to solve the problem.* Here are the pieces of information to work with:

(1) The task: *Find the unknown number of years it will take for Ms.Grande's ponytail length to equal her height*

(2) Initial hair length: *36 inches*

(3) Final hair length (*i.e.* Ms. Grande's height): *5 feet*

(4) Growth rate: *0.5 inches per month*

Not sure how these given pieces of information are related? Look for keywords associated with a rate because *rates* usually *relate* two of the variables.

Examples of keywords to look for are "per" or "each" or "for every." In this problem, the unit of the rate is inches *per* month, which relates the variables *length* and *time.* So, the growth rate of *0.5 inches per month* means that for every month that goes by, Ms. Grande's hair grows 0.5 inches. Furthermore, since the rate is constant, that means it is a *linear relationship*, so the rate also conveys the slope of the line, which will be an important fact later.

Before proceeding, a couple other things about the given information are worth noting:

- The keywords "how many" signal that the answer will be a number, and this can be confirmed by looking at the answer choices. Since the answer choices are numbers, we will potentially be able to use one of the alternative strategies mentioned in the previous sections, *backsolving*. This problem could have just as easily been presented as a grid-in problem though and required you to supply a numerical answer.

- The keywords "as long as" indicate the presence of an equivalency between two measures of length. In this problem, the equivalency will be between Ms. Grande's *hair length* and her *height*.

- The units for Ms. Grande's height and hair length, *feet* and *inches*, respectively, are not the same. You will need to convert one of those units at some point.

- The unit of time asked for in the task, *years*, is not present in the growth rate, *inches per month*. Another conversion will be needed there.

Now that you have gathered all the information in the problem and noticed the conversions you will need to make, you are ready for the next step. For most word problems, it is often helpful to *translate the given information into a mathematical equation*, which will then give you a direct path to the solution.

Consider the given information in this problem: *an initial length, a final length, an unknown time, and a constant rate that relates the change in length and time.* These are all the pieces of a linear equation that can be expressed in slope-intercept form: $y = mx + b$.

One side of the equation will be Ms. Grande's *final hair length* and the other side will tell us her *initial hair length* as well as *how it changes over time.* To find the answer, plug the given values into the equation and then solve for the unknown variable, *time.* Before doing that, however, determine the values associated with each of the variables.

First, b stands for the y-intercept, and in this problem, b is Ms. Grande's current ponytail length, *36 inches.* As a reminder, the y-intercept is the point at which a line crosses the y-axis, which is the vertical axis on a coordinate plane.

Another variable in the linear equation, m, represents the slope and is equal to the growth rate: *0.5 inches per month.* The slope tells you how quickly her hair length changes in relation to time, and the unit for the slope or rate in this problem is *inches* (hair length) *per month* (time).

Now that m and b are settled, what about the x- and y-variables in the linear equation that is being generated?

Time will almost always be the x-variable, which is sometimes referred to as the *independent variable*. The other variable, typically the y-variable, is called the *dependent variable* because it *depends upon* or is *determined by* the independent variable. If you have an equation that describes the relationship between the variables, like a linear equation, a value of x can be used to predict a value of y.

In this problem, time can be used to predict Ms. Grande's hair length, so time is the x-variable (*independent*) and hair length is the y-variable (*dependent*).

Let's quickly review again before proceeding:

- There is a linear relationship that can be expressed using slope-intercept form: $y = mx + b$

- b = initial hair length = 36 in

- m = growth rate = 0.5 in per month

- x = time = unknown

- y = final hair length = Ms. Grande's height = 5 ft

Notice anything that would be problematic if you were to plug those numbers into the linear equation and solve for x? Look at the units. The initial hair length and growth rate involve *inches* but the final hair length is in *feet. The unit of length used on both sides of the equation needs to be the same.* This is an *equation*, after all, so all aspects need to be *equal*, including the units. Since there is only one variable measured in *feet*, converting it to *inches* would be faster than converting the initial hair length *and* growth rate to feet and feet per month, respectively.

The final hair length is 5 feet, and since there are 12 inches per foot, do the following operation for that conversion:

$$y = 5 \times 12 \, \frac{in}{ft} = 60 \, in$$

Do you struggle with unit conversions? Here is a tool you can use. Draw (or imagine) a triangle with three sections arranged like the figure below, and then put a unit into each section.

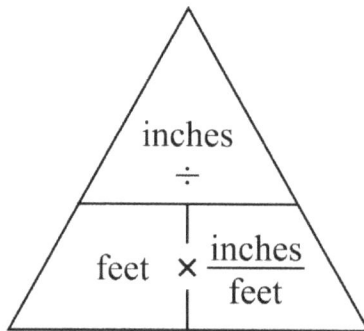

One of the bottom sections should have a unit that is a ratio of the two other units, like

$\frac{inches}{feet}$. Whichever unit is in the numerator of the ratio will be the unit that goes in the top section of the triangle.

In the conversion performed for hair length, feet need to be converted to *inches*. So, if you cover up the "inches" section with a finger, the following operation would remain uncovered:

$$feet \times \frac{inches}{feet}$$

That would therefore be the operation needed for the conversion. If you were needing to convert inches into *feet* instead, you would cover up the section with "feet" in it and then use the operation that remained uncovered:

$$inches \div \frac{inches}{feet}$$

This conversion tool for units also works for other rates or ratios made up of mixed dimensions, like miles per hour (distance per time) or miles per gallon (distance per volume) or grams per liter (mass per volume).

Now, you need to do the other conversion: changing the time component of the growth rate from $\frac{inches}{feet}$ to $\frac{inches}{year}$, so that the unit of time is consistent with the task, *years*. To do that, use the conversion factor, $12 \frac{months}{year}$, in the following operation:

$$m = 0.5 \frac{inches}{month} \times 12 \frac{months}{year} = 6 \frac{inches}{year}$$

Not sure when you should multiply or divide by a conversion factor? Look to the units to help you out. If you are beginning with $\frac{inches}{month}$ and need to convert it to $\frac{inches}{year}$, you need to multiply $\frac{inches}{month}$ by something that will cancel out the *months* and replace it with *years*. See below:

$$\frac{inches}{month} \times \frac{month}{year} = \frac{inches \times}{month \times} = \frac{inches \times \cancel{month}}{\cancel{month} \times year} = \frac{inches}{year}$$

When you multiply $\frac{inches}{month} \times \frac{months}{year}$, months will cancel out because it is present in both the numerator and denominator of the product. This leaves you with $\frac{inches}{year}$, which is the unit you want. So, in order to convert $0.5 \frac{inches}{month}$ to $\frac{inches}{year}$, you need to multiply it by, $12 \frac{months}{year}$ which gives you $6 \frac{inches}{year}$. If you were to divide $0.5 \frac{inches}{month}$ to $\frac{inches}{year}$ by, $12 \frac{months}{year}$ you would get $0.04167 \frac{inches \cdot year}{month^2}$, which is just a mess and obviously does not make sense.

Now that you have done both conversions, you are ready to plug everything into the equation, $y = mx + b$:

$$60 \ inches = (6 \ \frac{inches}{year})(x \ years) + 36 \ inches$$

You are approaching the end and have two options for your final steps:

(1) Solve for x algebraically

(2) Backsolve

You can backsolve because you have an equation as well as answer choices that are numbers. If you backsolve, you should start with answer choice (B) or (C) and assume that the x in your equation equals one of those choices. (B) is 4, so if you start with that choice, you would just plug 4 in for x, follow the order of operations, and see if both sides of the equation are equivalent. Here is what that would look like using $x = 4$:

$$60 = 6x + 36$$

$$60 = 6(4) + 36$$

$$60 = 24 + 36$$

$$60 = 60$$

Both sides are equivalent, so (B) is your answer!

If you solve for x algebraically, instead of backsolving, here is what that would look like:

$$60 = 6x + 36$$

$$60 - 36 = 6x + 36 - 36$$

$$24 = 6x$$

$$24 \div 6 = 6x \div 6$$

$$4 = x \ or \ x = 4$$

Done! $x = 4$, so (B) is the answer.

As you can see, both of these final series of steps get you to the same answer: *it will take 4 years for Ariana Grande's ponytail to grow to a length of 5 feet, which is answer choice* (B). Both final steps would also take about the same amount of time, so which method you choose really just comes down to personal preference on this problem. However, if the algebra had been a little more complex, backsolving would have probably been the faster method, even if you had not tested the correct answer choice on the first try.

Functions, Equations, or Inequalities

Perhaps more than any of the other question types on the test, these problems test your fundamental understanding of high school math skills and concepts. They are designed to test whether or not you possess the tools necessary to piece together a solution with only a few essential pieces of information. But fear not! These problems also tend to be great opportunities to use alternative strategies, like *backsolving* and *plugging in your own numbers*, even if they happen to be grid-in problems, like this example:

> If $x^2 - 2 < 6$ and $2x^2 + 1 > 7$, what is a possible value of x?

A lot of students are intimidated by inequality signs, but if you think about it, they should be less intimidating than equal signs because there is much less of a need to be exact. Equal signs suggest a specific solution (or occasionally a set of specific solutions), while inequalities typically indicate a *range* of solutions. For this problem, as long as you find a solution within the range that works for both inequalities, you will get it right.

With that in mind, let's dive in. First steps, isolate the x^2 in both inequalities.

$$x^2 - 2 < 6 \qquad\qquad 2x^2 + 1 > 7$$
$$x^2 < 8 \qquad\qquad 2x^2 > 6$$
$$x^2 > 3$$

You may be tempted to reach for your calculator at this point but resist that temptation. *You are not being asked to find the exact range of solutions.* You are being asked to find *a* solution *within that range,* and you do not need to know the square root of 8 or 3 to find a working solution. So, what do you do? Well, you know that x^2 is greater than 3 and less than 8. *Just plug in a number for x and see if it works.* What is 1^2? 1. That doesn't work. What is 2^2? 4. *Woohoo!* That is obviously between 3 and 8, so 2 is your answer. (Note: -2 would also work, but remember on grid-ins, the answer you fill in should always be a positive number.)

When given more than one equation or inequality, you do not always need to solve for a variable in one equation and then substitute that solution into the other, as that can sometimes require more steps than necessary. Before getting to that, however, here is a standard substitution problem that has no good shortcut:

If $y = 3x + 5$ and $x + 3 = 7$, what is y?

Solution: To solve for y, you first need to solve for x in the second equation, giving you $x = 4$. Next, you would just substitute 4 in for x in the first equation and then evaluate it:

$$y = 3x + 5 \Rightarrow y = 3(4) + 5 = 12 + 5 \Rightarrow y = 17$$

Again, in that problem, solving for x first could not be avoided. The next problem, however, shows that it is not always necessary to solve for x, which can save you precious time. Here it is:

If $x^2 + 6 = 14$, what is $3x^2 + 2$?

Solution: Instead of solving for x in the first equation and then plugging that into you just need to solve for x^2, like so:

$$x^2 + 6 = 14 \Rightarrow x^2 = 8$$

Next, simply substitute 8 in for x^2 in $3x^2 + 2$:

$$3x^2 + 2 \Rightarrow 3(8) + 2 \Rightarrow 24 + 2 \Rightarrow 26$$

Problems with Graphs or Tables

When you see a graph or table problem, you will likely be asked to *interpret the given data*, *identify a corresponding function or graph*, or *make a calculation* based on what is presented. These problems also have an increased likelihood of being extended thinking problems, with multiple questions for a single graph or table.

Tables contain data organized in rows and columns, like in the Taylor Swift problem earlier, while graphs show data visually and in a way that tends to be more easily interpretable. Some common types of graphs that tend to show up on the SAT Math Test are: line & bar graphs, pie charts, histograms, and scatterplots. Whether shown a table or graph, you should approach these problems in this methodical way:

(1) *Scan over the graph or table and learn the basics*

  a) What information is contained in the graph or table? (Look at the title, if present.)

  b) What are the variables and units on each axis (or in the columns and rows)?

  c) Are the variables related by a direct or inverse relationship?

  d) Is there a linear or exponential trend?

(2) *Read the prompt and identify the task*

(3) *Refer back to the graph or table and answer the question*

The example below is a problem that asks you to identify the graph that could most accurately represent the data presented in a table.

It is recommended that you try to picture the correct graph yourself first and then select the answer choice that is most similar to your own mental image. In other words, *backsolve as a last resort* on these problems. It is tempting to look at the graphs first and try to match the scenario to one of them, but it is more reliable to have your own vision of the graph *and then* match that to a choice.

SMS MESSAGES SENT IN THE U.S. ANNUALLY

Year	2005	2007	2009	2011	2013	2015
SMS sent (in billions)	80	360	1560	2300	2000	1850

The annual numbers of text messages (SMS) sent in the United States, 2005-2015 (odd years), are given in the table above. Which of the following graphs could represent the information in the table?

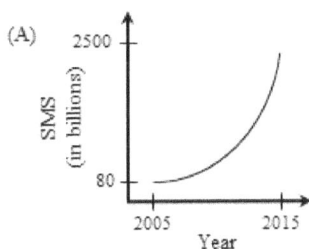

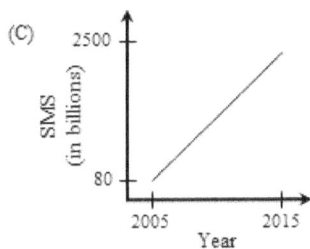

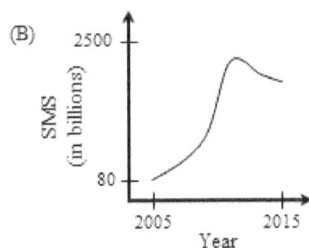

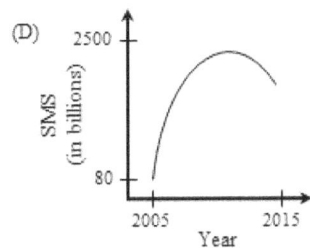

First step: Look over the table and learn the basics. The table shows the number of sent text messages in the United States between 2005 and 2015. Each column gives you a year and the number of text messages that were sent in that year.

Next step: Your task is to identify a graph that could represent the given data. This means you should look for any distinguishing characteristics or patterns or trends in the data. In particular, look for any peaks, troughs, rapid rises, rapid falls, positive trends, negative trends, and plateaus.

Final step: Looking through the table a little more closely, you should notice that there is a positive trend between 2005 and 2011 and a significant jump between 2007 and 2009. Then, the number of sent SMS messages decreases after 2011 and the rate of decrease slows between 2013 and 2015. At that point, you should have enough characteristics to identify the appropriate graph. Choices (A) and (C) can be easily eliminated because they never decrease. That leaves choices (B) and (D). Choice (B) looks to be the most consistent with the qualities identified earlier: a rapid jump about halfway through, a peak and then a decrease that almost levels out. Choice (D) would not work because it has a rapid increase starting at 2005, which is not consistent with the numbers in the table. (B) is the answer.

Problems with Figures or Diagrams

These problems will ask you a question (or maybe up to three) based on some two- or three-dimensional object that is shown. The common formulas and shapes shared on the reference page at the beginning of each math section will (unsurprisingly) be the most help to you on these questions. As with all problems, you should be prepared to use the alternative strategies described in the previous section, especially since Plugging in Your Own Numbers or Backsolving can often be much more efficient than The Natural on these problems.

It is also especially important to make note of all the given information on these problems, since all the postulates, theorems, and properties you learned in Geometry and Trigonometry should enable you to say more about a figure than is immediately apparent. For example, if you were given a right triangle that only showed you the lengths of two sides, you know that you could find the length of the third side using the Pythagorean Theorem, but you would only know that if you saw and made note of the given information.

With that in mind, here is the standard way to approach problems with a figure or diagram:

(1) *Look over the figure, making note of the given and missing pieces of information*

(2) *Read the prompt and identify the task*

(3) *Mark up (or redraw, if necessary) the figure, including the missing pieces of information you need to find the answer*

(4) *Find the answer*

You can be assume that figures are drawn to scale unless there is a statement next to the figure that says, "Note: Figure not drawn to scale." If you see that statement, it can often be helpful to *redraw* the figure, since the unscaled drawing can sometimes make incorrect answers appear correct or obscure accurate relationships between sides or angles.

The example below illustrates the procedure for solving these types of problems.

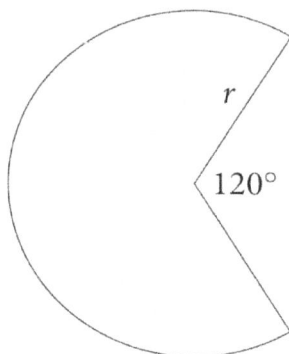

After eating a power pellet, Pac-Man, a circular maze-dwelling creature from the 1980s, knows he must open his mouth at least 120° in order to eat a ghost with height, h. At that point, the opening of his mouth will equal the height of the ghost and enable him to swallow the ghost whole. If Pac-Man has a radius of r, what does h equal in terms of r?

(A) $\dfrac{r\sqrt{3}}{2}$

(B) $2r\sqrt{3}$

(C) $r\sqrt{3}$

(D) $\dfrac{r\sqrt{3}}{3}$

First step: After looking over the figure, you should see that the figure has a central angle of 120° and a radius of r. Next, in the prompt, you are told that the opening has a length of h.

Second step: Your task is to find an expression for h in terms of r.

Third step: Now is when you should mark up the figure with the information that will help you find the answer. See the marked up figure below:

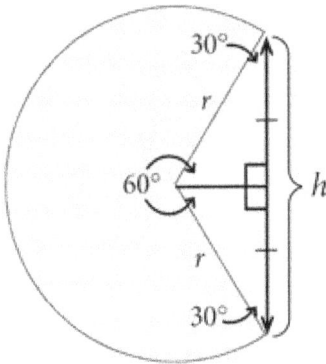

Draw a line for h that extends across the opening, then bisect the 120° angle, which gives you two 60° angles. Since you were told that r was a radius, the other segment extending from the center must also be a radius.

From the marked up figure, you can see that you now have two congruent 30-60-90 triangles with hypotenuse, r. The length of the long leg for each triangle would just be the height of the opening, h, divided by 2. However, if you look at the answer choices, there are no other variables present other than *r*, so you know that the radius is the only variable you need. *How do you get from r to an expression of h?* One step at a time.

Refer to the figure to see the next steps.

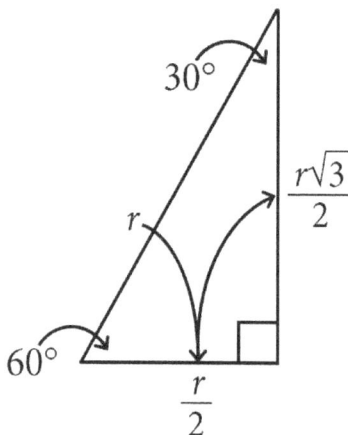

Reminder: A sample 30-60-90 triangle is shown on the reference page at the beginning of the test section.

Using your knowledge of 30-60-90 triangles, determine the length of the short leg:

$$r \div 2 = \frac{r}{2}$$

Now, find the long leg in terms of *r*:

$$\frac{r}{2} \times \sqrt{3} = \frac{r\sqrt{3}}{2}$$

Final step! Going off the marked up Pac-Man figure, the two long legs together make up *h*, so you just need to multiply the long leg, $\frac{r\sqrt{3}}{2}$, by 2:

$$\frac{r\sqrt{3}}{2} \times 2 = r\sqrt{3}$$

Done! The answer is (C).

If you are not sure how to get started on working *toward* the answer, as shown above, try reverse engineering the problem, working backwards from the variable you are looking for. For the above problem, that would mean working backwards from *h* to *r*. Keep in mind that *h* spans the entire mouth of Pac-Man, so half of *h* is just *h* divided by 2. Here is how that would work:

According to the marked up Pac-Man figure, the length of the long leg of each triangle is half the length of *h*, or $\frac{h}{2}$.

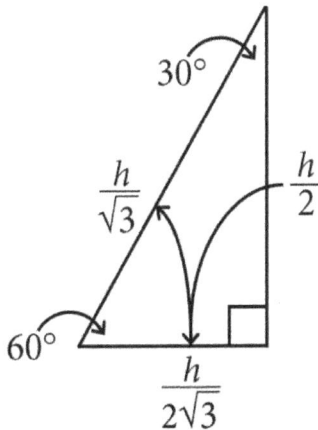

Continuing in that direction and using your knowledge of 30-60-90 triangles, you would eventually arrive at $r = \frac{h}{\sqrt{3}}$. Your last step would just be to multiply both sides of that equation by $\sqrt{3}$, ending up with an equation for h in terms of r: $h = r\sqrt{3}$, or choice (C).

HOW DO I PREPARE FOR THE MATH SECTIONS?

Getting started with your preparations early means that you are more likely to get the score you want on your first try. What follows is a suggested timeline for your test preparation.

3+ Months Out: Practice, Plan, and Begin to Prepare

Take a practice test. The College Board has several free practice SATs available for download on their website. Use them. Learn the strategies in this book and practice using them under test-like conditions. Taking a test early on will help you to:

(1) become familiar with the test's directions, structure, and question types

(2) identify content areas that you struggle with

(3) determine if your pace needs hastening

Work on your problem areas. After taking your first practice test, you will likely identify some areas in need of improvement. If you struggle on particular topics, like finding arc lengths or solving systems of equations, those are areas you should focus on. The more strengths you have, the more efficient and accurate you will be while taking the test.

Less than 3 months to go

Do problem-solving drills. Go through four or five practice problems at a time, marking them up and determining how you would approach each problem, *but do not actually work through them yet.* The point of this activity is to get practice visualizing the steps and choosing the best strategies. Once you have gone through a set or two in this way, go back and actually work through the problems, making note of the ones where your initial strategy did not work or was too time-consuming. Those are problems you should try again in the future.

Create your own math problems. Many of the SAT Math problems are based in real-world contexts, so start coming up with problems based on your own real-life experiences. For example, if you are going somewhere across town, turn it into a math problem: If you walk six minutes to the bus stop and take the bus 12 miles across town at an average speed of 25 miles per hour, how long will the total travel time be, in minutes, starting from the moment you leave the house? The point is to get more practice thinking mathematically. This will greatly improve your problem-solving skills, just like reading a newspaper will help improve your comprehension and critical reading skills.

Train your internal clock. You have about 75 seconds per problem, which means you should be able to complete four problems every five minutes. Find official practice problems on the College Board website and use a timer to do five-minute drills, attempting to complete four problems in five minutes. To make it more fun, create a playlist of songs that are all about five-minutes long and do some drills. Practicing in this way will help you to find your rhythm before test day, and you will learn to feel when you are on- or off-pace.

Understand your mistakes. Content that used to challenge you should be more manageable at this point. When you get a practice problem wrong, however, rework it without looking at the explanation of the answer. If you still get it wrong, read the explanation, and then *rework it again.* By *actively* working through a problem in the correct way, you are much less likely to make the same error again than if you were to *passively* read the explanation.

Practice how you will perform. Take at least two more full practice tests in the last month before your test. These will reveal what areas you still need to work on and whether your pacing strategy is enabling you to finish the test within the time limits.

Do something every day. In the final few weeks leading up to test day, plan on doing something, even if it is just doing a five-minute drill or reworking some difficult problems right before you go to bed. Every little bit will help keep the essential concepts, skills and strategies fresh in your mind.

FIGURES, FACTS, AND FORMULAS TO REMEMBER

Below are the figures, facts, and formulas that you will see at the beginning of each math section.

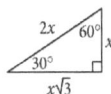

$A = \pi r^2$ $A = \ell w$ $A = \frac{1}{2}bh$ $c^2 = a^2 + b^2$ Special Right Triangles
$C = 2\pi r$

$V = \ell wh$ $V = \pi r^2 h$ $V = \frac{4}{3}\pi r^3$ $V = \frac{1}{3}\pi r^2 h$ $V = \frac{1}{3}\ell wh$

The number of degrees of arc in a circle is 360.

The number of radians of arc in a circle is 2π.

The sum of the measures in degrees of the angles of a triangle is 180.

Below are the figures, facts, and formulas not given on the reference page but recommended you remember. They are organized by content area.

Heart of Algebra

Slope formula. If you ever need to calculate the slope of line between two given points (x_1, y_1) and (x_2, y_2), use this formula:

$$slope = m = \frac{rise\ (change\ in\ y)}{run\ (change\ in\ x)} = \frac{y2 - y1}{x2 - x1}$$

Perpendicular slopes. If a line intersects another line at a right angle, then its slope is the *negative reciprocal* of the other line. For example, if line 1 has a slope of 4 and it intersects line 2 at a right angle, the slope of line 2 is the negative reciprocal of 4, or $-\frac{1}{4}$.

Parallel slopes. Lines that never intersect have equal slopes.

Linear equations. There are three forms of linear equations you should know and be able to manipulate:

(1) slope-intercept form: $y = mx + b$

(2) point-slope form: $y - y1 = m(x - x1)$

(3) standard form: $Ax + By = C$

Midpoint formula. Use this formula to find the midpoint between two points on a line:

$$midpoint = (\frac{(x1 + x2)}{2}, \frac{(y1 + y2)}{2})$$

Distance formula. To find the distance between two points in a coordinate plane, use this formula:

$$distance = \sqrt{(x2 - x1)^2 + (y2 - y1)^2}$$

Average speed. The average speed of an object is the total distance traveled divided by the total time spent traveling. Here is its formula:

$$average\ speed = \frac{total\ distance}{total\ time}$$

Absolute values. These can really complicate an inequality problem if you do not know these three things:

(1) If $|x|=3$, then $x = 3$ or $x = -3$

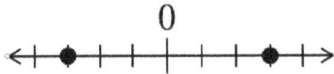

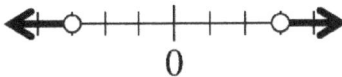

$$0$$

(2) If $|x|<3$, then $-3 < x < 3$

$$0$$

(3) If $|x|>3$, then $x < -3$ or $x > 3$

$$0$$

Problem Solving & Data Analysis

Exponential growth and decay. There are a few different formulas for growth and decay that you should remember and know when to apply. (A = ending amount, P = principal or starting amount, r = rate of growth/decay, t = time, n = number of periods)

(1) general form: $A=P(1 \pm r)^t$

(2) continuous growth/decay: $A=Pe^{rt}$

(3) compounding growth/decay: $A=P(1 \pm \frac{r}{n})$

Percent change. These problems can be tricky, so do them in steps, and think about them in terms of initial/final, before/after or new/old to get them set up.

$$\text{percent change} = \frac{final - initial}{initial} \times 100\%$$

Probability. Calculate the likelihood that an event will occur by taking the number of ways that the desired event can occur and dividing that by the total number of possible events. For example, if you flip a coin, there are two possible events or outcomes: heads or tails. What is the probability of the coin landing on heads?

$$\text{Probability of heads} = \frac{number\ of\ ways\ heads\ can\ occur}{total\ number\ of\ possible\ outcomes} = \frac{1}{2}$$

Passport to Advanced Math

Quadratic Equations. A quadratic equation is an equation that has a term with an exponent of 2. They can be expressed in two ways that you should know:

(1) standard form: $y = ax^2 + bx + c$

(2) vertex form: $y = a(x - h)^2 + k$, where (h, k) is the vertex

Vertex of a parabola. This is a very useful formula for finding the point at which the path of a parabola changes directions.

$$x = \frac{-b}{2a}$$

Common quadratic equations. These are good to know because they can save you time on challenging problems. They are especially helpful when attempting to factor or simplify a rational expression.

(1) $(x + y)(x - y) = x^2 - y^2$

(2) $(x + y)2 = x^2 + 2xy + y^2$

(3) $(x - y)^2 = x^2 - 2xy + y^2$

Quadratic formula:

$$x = \frac{-b \pm \sqrt{b^2 - 4ac}}{2a}$$

Additional Topics in Math

3-4-5 Special Right Triangle. In addition to the 30-60-90 and 45-45-90 special right triangles, a good one to know is the 3-4-5 right triangle. The legs and hypotenuse of this triangles adhere to a 3:4:5 ratio. So, if you identify such a right triangle, rather than calculating the third side using the Pythagorean theorem, you can just use the special ratio. Below are a couple examples of these triangles.

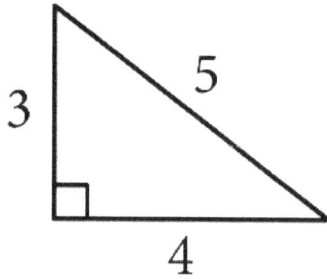

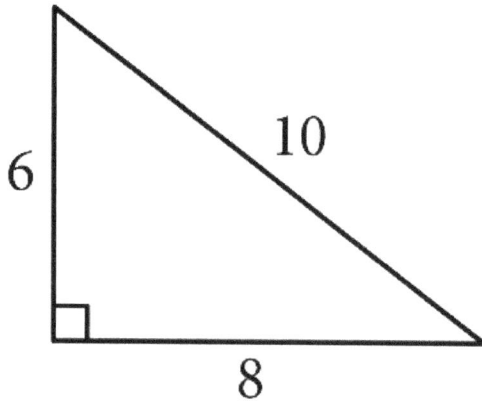

Triangle inequality rule. The length of a side of a triangle must be less than the sum of the lengths of the other two sides. Knowing this rule should help you to eliminate answer choices or find an answer by plugging in your numbers.

Degree to radian conversions. Remember this fact: *360 degrees equals 2π radians.* Be prepared to do a conversion using that fact. For example, here is how you would convert 45 degrees into radians:

$$45° \times \frac{2\pi\ radians}{360°} = \frac{\pi}{4}\ radians$$

Arc lengths. An arc is a portion of a circle's *circumference (2πr)*, and an arc length, L, is proportional to the angle of the arc divided by the total number of degrees in a circle, 360. You can use this proportion on problems involving arc lengths.

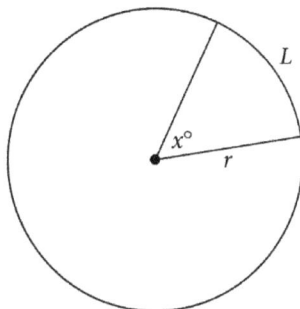

$$\frac{L}{2\pi r} = \frac{x°}{360°}$$

Sector areas. A sector is like a slice of pizza and refers to a part of the total *area of a circle (πr²)*. Like the arc length, a sector area, A, is also proportional to the angle of the arc divided by 360 degrees.

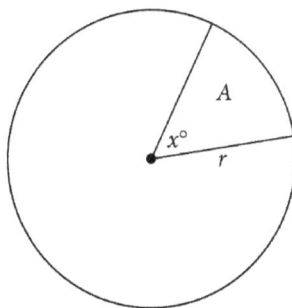

$$\frac{A}{\pi r^2} = \frac{x°}{360°}$$

Trigonometric ratios. Remember *SOHCAHTOA?* Good! You will likely need it on a couple problems.

$$\text{Sine} = \frac{Opposite}{Hypotenuse}$$

$$\text{Cosine} = \frac{Adjacent}{Hypotenuse}$$

$$\text{Tangent} = \frac{Opposite}{Adjacent}$$

Vertical angles theorem. When two lines intersect, the angles opposite each other are congruent. In the figure below, angles 1 & 3 are congruent and angles 2 & 4 are congruent.

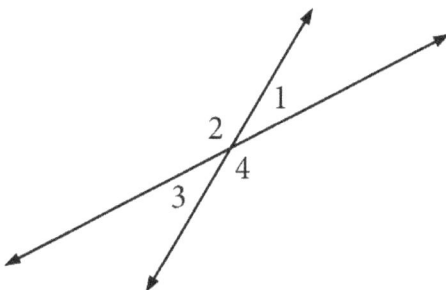

4.
The Essay Section

The SAT Essay Test, given at the end of the SAT, is optional for all students yet still required by many colleges.

The test asks you to compose an essay analyzing a short argumentative passage.

You have 50 minutes to complete the test.

The passage is different with each exam, but the prompts are basically the same.

You will be shown this prompt *before* the passage:

As you read the passage below, consider how [the author] uses

evidence, such as facts or examples, to support claims.

reasoning to develop ideas and to connect claims and evidence.

stylistic or persuasive elements, such as word choice or appeals to emotion to add power to the ideas expressed.

Your will be shown this prompt *after* the passage:

Write an essay in which you explain how [the author] builds an argument to persuade [his/her] audience that [the author's claim]. In your essay, analyze how [the author] uses one or more of the features listed above (or features of your own choice) to strengthen the logic and persuasiveness of [his/her] argument. Be sure that your analysis focuses on the most relevant features of the passage.

Your essay should not explain whether you agree with [the author's] claims, but rather explain how the author builds an argument to persuade [his/her] audience.

Your scores for the test will be reported separately and are not factored into your Reading and Writing Score.

You will receive three scores judged on a 2-8 scale: Reading, Analysis, and Writing.

Your Reading score judges your understanding of the passage, and is assessed by questions such as the following:

How well do you understand the main idea, the most import-

ant details, and how they inter-relate?

How well do you show this with textual evidence, such as quotes and paraphrases?

Are there any errors or misunder-standings in how you represent the text?

Your Analysis score judges your ability to explain how the author builds his/her argument. It is assessed by questions such as the following:

How well do you evaluate how the author builds his/her argument with evidence, reasoning, and sty-listic or persuasive elements?

How well do you support your claims?

Your Writing score judges the written quality of your essay. The basis of this judgment is more complex than the others, and it will be discussed in de-tail in a later section.

HOW DO I DO IT?

Corresponding to the three scores, there are three main tasks in tackling the SAT essay test: Reading, Analyzing, and Writing:

I. Read

Step One: Look at the final prompt of the passage to find out what the conclusion of the argument is.

Step Two: With the conclusion in mind, read the passage while using your pencil to mark anything that helps persuade the reader of the conclusion.

- Write notes in the margins.

- Underline potential quotations.

Look out for:

Evidence, such as:

(1) Statistics or data

"There were an average of 14 flu-related deaths in Altuna County for the 2014-15 flu season.

(2) Examples and case studies

"One elderly gentleman, Mr. Ronald MacDonald, died in the county hospital the day before his 80th birthday."

(3) Relevant facts

"Influenza can be spread by airborne droplets, skin contact, or other forms of contamination."

(4) Authoritative sources

> "According to Francisco Martinez, Professor of Immunology at the University of Altoona, flu shots will likely become even more effective in years to come."

Arguments, such as:

(1) Induction: A generalizing or predictive conclusion is supported by particular cases or examples.

> "In 1988, the government of Solville was violating the terms of the treaty; in 1998, they continued to violate the treaty; in 2008, they were still violating the treaty. It is thus very likely that they will violate the treaty in 2018."

(2) Argument by Analogy: One situation is alleged to have a certain property based on its similarity to another situation that also has that property.

> "If certain drugs are illegal because they have been shown to cause brain damage, shouldn't football, which has also been shown to cause brain damage, likewise be illegal?"

(3) Counterargument: A point of view is supported by refuting opposing arguments or alternative positions.

"In opposition to my view, many have argued that the best strategy is a preemptive attack. But this has the obvious downside of alienating potential allies, who may conclude that we played the role of instigator in this conflict."

(4) Argument by Elimination: A point of view is proven by identifying it as one of several possible options and then ruling out all the others.

"Either we attack by water, air, or land. We have no navy, so we cannot attack by water. We have no air force, so we cannot attack by air. Therefore, we will attack by land!"

(5) *Reductio ad absurdum* ("reduction to absurdity"): A point of view is proven by showing that its denial leads to something impossible or otherwise unacceptable.

"God exists, because if God does not exist, then all things would be permitted, and it's obviously false that all things are permitted."

Stylistic or persuasive devices, such as:

(6) Appeal to Authority: Sometimes called *ethos*, this device tries to establish the trustworthiness of the author, or a source of information, by appealing to the respectability of the individual or institution in question.

"As someone with a PhD in Educational Psychology and a career in higher education lasting more than 25 years, I have come to know a lot about the best techniques for classroom instruction."

(7) Appeal to Emotion: Sometimes called *pathos*, this device tries to persuade the reader by appealing to pity, fear or any other compelling emotion.

"If we don't act decisively and immediately, the results will be horrific, leading to millions of deaths, and there will be no one to blame but ourselves."

(8) Mob Appeal: An attempt to persuade by appealing to group identification.

"These matters might seem complicated, but there is only one choice for the true patriot here. If you love your country, you must stand by her decisions at this time."

(9) Narrative Persuasion: Use of story-telling to create identification, sympathy, or other persuasive effect.

> "... and when I was finally saved from that underground jail in the jungle of Vietnam, I knew that if I would never vote to defund our great military. I urge you to do the same."

(10) Self-Revelation: Use of a personal voice to establish a sense of trust, familiarity or identification with the reader conducive to persuasion.

> "You have all known me from the beginning, ever since my son Joey was born right here in this city. It was then that I began my long war against corruption in our government.

(11) Diction and Figures of Speech: Use of colorful or evocative language, including similes and metaphors, to create mood or otherwise persuade the reader.

> "... I knew America would never invest the necessary funds or energies in rehabilitation of its poor so long as adventures like Vietnam continued to draw men and skills and money like some demonic destructive suction tube."

(12) Tone: Use of authorial attitude, such as outrage, sarcasm, or irony, to persuasive effect.

"...I could never again raise my voice against the violence of the oppressed in the ghettos without having first spoken clearly to the greatest purveyor of violence in the world today – my own government. For the sake of those boys, for the sake of this government, for the sake of the hundreds of thousands trembling under our violence, I cannot be silent."

II. Analyze

Now that you've read and annotated the prompt essay, you are ready to begin analyzing this information and outlining your own essay. Here's how:

Step One: *Identify your main points.* Look over your notes and determine the most important evidence, reasoning, and stylistic or persuasive devices used in the passage to support the conclusion.

Determine the importance of a point not just by the amount of space an author dedicates to it but also by how relevant it is to supporting the conclusion.

Step Two: *Identify your subordinate points.* Consider the remaining evidence, reasoning, and stylistic or persuasive devices, and reflect on how these might play a role in advancing the points you identified in step one.

For example, if a statistical point about the economic efficiency of solar power is developed by using stylistic devices such as story telling or figures of speech, include this in your discussion of the former.

Step Three: *Organize your points.* Identify the ideal logical ordering of all your points and compose a brief outline.

Often, it will make sense to follow the order of the passage, but you may want to alter this to emphasize some significant logical connection between your points.

Step Four: *Compose your thesis sentence.* A good thesis sentence (a) makes a judgment and (b) explains briefly why that judgment is correct. It is your essay boiled down to one sentence and serves as a mini outline.

"In his wide ranging discussion, Kintaro makes effective use of statistical data, a compelling argument by analogy, and several stylistic devices to persuade the reader of the superiority of a vegetarian diet."

III. Write

Your final task is to turn what you've read and analyzed into a well-written essay that answers the prompt. Here's how:

Step One: Introduction

(1) *Hook:* Engage the reader, introduce the topic, and establish context by briefly talking about the subject of the passage in a general way.

Some strategies:

> Bold statements: "It's very possible that the grandchildren of anyone reading these words will live in a world in which famine, disease, and the effects of geopolitical instability will have made daily life a brute struggle for survival."

> Provocatively stated questions: "How long can our leaders deny the advice of 98 percent of all university scientists? How long can we let our country be governed by corrupt and incompe-

tent politicians who cater only to corporate interests? How long can we, the voting public, remain immobilized by our indifference?"

(2) *Transition to thesis:* Introduce the text, mentioning its title and the author's name, stating how it addresses the problem expressed in the hook.

"But if Patrick Malawi is right, there is still hope. In his New York Times article, 'We're Completely Doomed Unless We Act Now,' Malawi persuasively argues that the way to secure our future is through immediate legislative acts limiting CO_2 emissions resulting from industrial production processes."

(3) *Thesis:* A brief statement of your analysis of the text. Remember, a good thesis (a) makes a judgment and (b) says why:

"Malawi contends vigorously for his view by appealing to the opinions of well established authorities in and outside the sciences, by marshaling an impressive array of supporting facts, including statistical and other data, and finally by anticipating and refuting an important objection to his thesis."

Step Two: Body

Write one paragraph for each of your main points:

First Body Paragraph:

(1) Opening Sentence: Start with a strong transitional sentence stating the main point of the paragraph.

"Malawi begins his essay by citing a variety of well established scientists to support his view."

(2) Supporting Point #1: Provide an example, quotation, paraphrase, or other textual reference that exemplifies the general point you are making.

"For example, he quotes the opinion of Dr. Raymond Seborg, Nobel Laureate and Chair of the UCLA department of Geology, who asserts that current rates of global warming are only sustainable for 30 more years before we will encounter 'a tipping point that will rapidly and irreversibly alter life on planet earth.'"

(3) Analysis of Point #1: Talk about how this evidence supports the general point you are making

"By appealing to the opinion of someone so well respected in the scientific world, Malawi shows that his view, alarming though it might be, is not the eccentric opinion of some radical minority but one held by widely respected experts."

(4) Supporting Point #2: If available, provide a second example, quotation, paraphrase or other textual reference that exemplifies the general point you are making.

"Besides Seborg, Malawi also quotes the striking remark of UN Chief Officer of Global Tragedy, Helmut Kung, that the problem cannot be solved without the 'active and continued legislative and financial involvement' of the world's leading nation-states."

(5) Analysis of Point #2: Talk about how this evidence supports the general point you are making.

"Although Kung is not a scientist, quoting such a well respected leader in global politics helps further establish the *ethos* of Malawi's own views by illustrating that they have taken hold outside the world of science."

(6) Closing Sentence: Sum up the paragraph by relating your discussion of evidence to the main point you are making.

"In quoting such a diversity of sources Malawi successfully establishes the initial credibility of his view about the urgency of anti-CO_2 legislation by showing it has the backing of the kinds of experts who are in a position to know about such things."

Paragraphs 2 & 3

Start additional paragraphs with strong transitions that relate what you are saying now to what you have said before:

"Not only does Malawi appeal to authoritative sources to support his view, he also makes direct use of fact, data, and statistics to convince the reader..."

Repeat the procedure above for as many points as you have to make.

Step Three: Conclusion

A good conclusion will clearly and memorably summarize what has been said.

Here's how:

(1) Restate the main points of your body paragraphs by putting them together with a meta-thesis (a thesis about your thesis): say something about how they hang together, or just emphasize your evaluation of the passage.

"Like weaving a powerful braid, Patrick Malawi makes a strong three-part case for the urgency of immediate legislative action limiting CO_2 emissions. He accomplishes this by intertwining the effective quotation of a diversity of respected authorities with direct evidence in the form of quantifiable factual data, as well as with refutations of an important objection from the opposition."

(2) Use the following tools to help keep the rest of your conclusion fresh and energized:

Allude to the Hook: *Lead into* presenting your summary of your argument by making reference to your hook:

Before the sentence above, write: "The problems of climate change are not going away anytime soon. What should be done? If Patrick Malawi is right, one part of the solution is that that legislators must act immediately."

Call to Action: *End* by expressing your agreement with the author and joining in with his/her call to action.

"Any reader with a conscience comes away from this argument feeling not just persuaded but motivated and inspired to advocate for these important legislative changes."

General Writing Tips

Here's how the readers will determine your Writing score, along with some tips for making sure you get it right:

Concept and Organization

Is your essay cohesive?

Stay on topic and use transitional words and phrases to take the reader with you.

Remember: the topic is the essay you are analyzing, not your own opinions on the subject.

Does it contain a precise central claim?

> Compose a clear thesis statement and argue for it.

Is there a clear progression of ideas (in paragraphs and as a whole) in support of the central claim?

> Logically organize your main points and evidence to support your thesis. Use an outline.

Does the essay include a skillful introduction and conclusion?

> Follow the advice above for composing introductions and conclusions.

Writing and Style

Do you demonstrate an effective use and command of language?

> Test your sentences by speaking them aloud (or, if in a public testing situation, saying them 'out loud' in your head).

Does the essay employy precise word choice?

> If you can find a more ~~precise~~ apposite word, use it, but ~~eschew gratuitous sesquipedalianism~~ avoid unnecessary use of long words,

and always avoid using words you don't really ~~cogitate~~ know.

Does the essay employ a variety of sentence structure?

Avoid repetitive sentence openings; vary the length of your sentences; artfully alternate simple, compound, and complex sentences.

Does the essay employ a formal style and objective tone?

Avoid first-person pronouns and self-references (e.g., "In my opinion"), emotive language, pejoratives, slang, and jokes.

Does the essay adhere to the conventions of standard written English?

See our SAT Writing & Language Section for more on this.

Expert Test Taking Tips

Write neatly. Write as legibly as you can. If your cursive is illegible, print. If your printing is illegible, use CAPITALS (enlarging specific letters to show actual capitals).

Manage your time wisely.

As a general rule, aim to start writing with at least 30 minutes to go. Times vary for each individual and each exam, but you likely should spend 4-8 minutes reading, 6-10 minutes analyzing and outlining, 25-35 minutes writing, and 2 minutes proofreading.

Use leftover time to correct errors, improve word choice, and check the legibility of your writing.

If you run out of time, finish what you are writing as well as you can rather than rush carelessly through to the end.

Start strong. Make sure your introduction is good; first impressions can be decisive.

Pump up the volume. Skip lines between paragraphs in order to show readers the structure of your essay and to amplify length. On average, longer essays = higher scores. Aim for at least two pages.

HOW DO I PREPARE FOR THE ES-SAY TEST?

Now that you know what's necessary for succeeding on the SAT Essay Test, all that's left to do is prepare.

Here's how:

Follow the general guidelines in the section of this book called How to Prepare for the SAT.

If you have three months or more:

> Take regular practice tests, although take them less frequently than you would in the three months leading up to the test (perhaps once a week).

> Read lots of quality non-fiction writing, such as what you might find in the *New York Times* (especially the Op-ed section), the *New Yorker*, and the *Economist*, and practice analyzing how these authors make their arguments.

If you have less than three months until the test:

> Work through this chapter and make sure you thoroughly understand all the principles of reading, analysis and composition discussed here.

> Take at least 2 practice tests per week; work until the many steps laid out in this guide become automatic to you.

> Hire an experienced SAT tutor to evaluate your essays and give you feedback.

> Seek out and analyze sample 8-8-8 SAT essays.

Hampton Tutors is an academic coaching and tutoring agency based in Seattle, WA.

We build intellectual skills, confidence, and enjoyment of learning. This comes through helping students develop Executive Function and metacognition alongside their subject-specific work.

We believe strongly in teaching both content and processes to help students with their work. That means showing them how to do specific problems, but also how to solve similar problems in the future.

We provide unique, tailored coaching for students, either one-on-one or in small group settings. To find out more about what we offer, contact us at:

hello@hamptontutors.com

206.693.4101

www.hamptontutors.com

www.ingramcontent.com/pod-product-compliance
Lightning Source LLC
Chambersburg PA
CBHW030842090426
42737CB00009B/1072